FAITH

Over

Fear

By: StarSpeaks

ISBN-13: 978-0692435724

DEDICATION:

This book is dedicated to my <u>Daddy</u>, **Bird.**
I thank him for tapping into my passion. He was my first pen pal, lol. My first fan, supporter, and motivator. My first love!! He allowed me to see things that I couldn't or wouldn't allow myself to see. Beyond what they could see, he brought out the emotion in me. Tried his best to allow me to feel each one. He always told me the truth & allowed me to deal with it. Most of all...he poured love into me. Taught my soul how to feel. He was my communication. *"Thanks for believing in me, writing to me, challenging me...For appreciating & aweing my beauty. Laughing at my goofy, my crazy, and my weirdness. For accepting the being I am. Our love was beyond what they could see. I was me & you were you"*. Freedom was what we were into & that's what I felt with him. *"I'll stay close to the gift you pushed out of me. Fly often to feel your spirit. And look daily at a reflection of a beauty you helped create. How can I miss your presence when it's so strong around me? We could never be separated! Now that you've been freed, it's my turn!"* Rest in peace Daddy!! Love you mostest.

Table of CONTENTS:

<u>To ALL of my children:</u>

Life will bring many things. Some are valuable, some may not
be worth a second look. You will always go through things!
Everything happens for a reason & or a lesson. It's important to
know where your help comes from. Remember that there is NO
BOX!! So, there's no need to step outside of something that
doesn't exist. No one can place limits or boundaries on your
gifts, talents, and treasures! Your future has endless, powerful
& meaningful possibilities! People will come and go. That's why
God made seasons! One thing for sure is that Mother Nature is
always present! Whether seen or felt! I believe in you, I support
you, I'm here for you, ALWAYS. A family is a group of people
who love each other unconditionally!! Our love is infinite! I
pray that you all go after your dreams and passions & follow
your heart! Love you mostest!!

ABOUT...

In this book you will find all kinds of emotions. I realized that my fears were overpowering my existence. Everything I did fear was my captive. _Fear_ is powerful & controlling BUT _FAITH_ is prevailing and authoritative!! Once you realize that faith and fear CANNOT coexist. Once you realize that God made us in his image & fear isn't one of the components...things begin to be clearer. Like needing glasses. Sometimes bifocals, but uhm...yeah (lol). I have paired these poems up to be like a storm turning into a brighter day. Or heartbreak turning into peace or acceptance. You will be up, down, in & out of love, depressed & uplifted!! Every experience isn't my own, some are merely observances. You can try to figure out which ones pertain to me if you like. Or you can see where they reflect you or someone you know. Learn from them. Love them. Heal with them. I hope you enjoy a piece of my soul.

Star Speaks

StarSpeaks,
And I'm loud & clear.
I'm tired of being bound by fear!
So, I'll sit right here.
Look me straight in the mirror &
turn it multi directional.
Looking outward & deep in the middle.
Check my surroundings &
keep all my findings.
Mellow in a memory &
put me down in history.
Where they tried to shame me.
But I've found me,
by searching for him.
I no longer have to accept being bound by them!
I've learned my lessons &
accepted my blessings.
People have always talked,
but now…
StarSpeaks

<u>ALONE & SCARED</u>

Alone and scared,

every time I go in there.

Nervous & shaken,

and no one seems to care.

I'll just bow my head in

prayer,

Lord free me like the air.

Show my purpose,

give me the courage.

Replace the fear with faith.

Allow me to take my place.

As I stand tall with grace,

my shine shows your glow proving humility.

You've placed strength in me,

so that I could believe.

·Star Speaks

<u>*EVERYDAY*</u>

Everyday...

I must remember,

that I have something special.

Something worth fighting for!

I have a gift that I must use,

a hand I'm meant to hold.

Someone I should get to know.

Some, I'll have to let go.

Most importantly,

I'm meant to be my greatest!

That alone...

is my motivation.

Star Speaks

___BROKEN___

I wanna give but what do I have?

I'm just broken,

no one's token.

Shattered,

heart just battered.

Swept away,

with nothing to say.

Discarded,

physically tired,

and mentally guarded.

Why?!

How?!

Where do I go from here?!

Is there a way to heal?!

My treatment starts with me.

Lord, I pray for the strength I need,

to fix me!

Star Speaks

MEANT TO BE

I wanna be someone's meant to be!

Their happily ever after!

Behind God, I'm their first and last,

beginning and ending.

I wanna see the attraction in our faces.

Compliments in all the right places,

I'm the reason he smiles when at peace,

the biggest prize in his eyes!

I wanna feel like I'm wanted,

and needed.

You know, well treated.

I wanna be all theirs,

and know that they're all mine!

Just the perfect find.

I wanna be a best friend,

I wanna be the end,

of the games,

the lames...

I wanna be the only fit to their puzzle.

Not perfect ourselves but our fit is for each other,

Forever.

*Star Speaks

I PAY

I pay attention in class.

Not because I'm a geek or nerd.

I want to hear something I've never heard.

Be beyond the present & connect with the past.

I've gotta pay attention in class.

To have a brighter tomorrow,

a lesser chance to attract sorrow.

I want to be one of the best!

So I will ace this test!

I pay attention,

to my surroundings,

and elaborate on my findings.

When it's asked, I wanna be the one to mention.

I pay...

for my decisions & my actions.

So, I take notes & ask questions.

Listen so I know what to say &

inevitably get paid!!

Star Speaks

<u>SITUATION CHANGED</u>

My situation has changed.

Change turned into dollars

and things finally made sense.

You need sense to make dollars,

so, I gave dollars to a good cause.

And the cause turned into a chance,

and the chance received an education.

This in return came back to me,

because I was thanked for the opportunity.

I had sense enough to invest,

in something that gives others,

the chance to make dollars.

Star Speaks

GUILTY

I'm guilty...

I'm guilty of needing people.

Of letting them take advantage of me.

Letting them abuse what's free.

I'm guilty...

of being afraid,

scared that I'll end up alone.

That my dreams will go un-shown.

Nervous I'll hurt myself,

before I've finished my test.

I'm guilty of praying,

for a rewind or a new beginning.

A pause to look around at the situation.

To change that first question.

Yeah, that's me, I'm guilty!

Of learning to accept God,

of learning to love myself!

Of accepting quiet time for me,

just so that I can think.

I'm guilty...yeah I am,

of starting over.

Star Speaks

TOO GUILTY

I'm guilty...
guilty of being too flirtatious,

too mean,

too nice,

too me.

I'm guilty!

Completely!

Of thinking about me,

strong willed & minded.

So hard I can't hide it.

I'm guilty of second chances.

As well as fencing in and bracing my heart.

Yet, still loving from the start.

Of meaning what I say.

Of profoundly procrastinating,

of just taking all day!

Terribly guilty of being hilarious,

and being so darn right!

Yeah...that's me,

Guilty!!

*Star Speaks

TROUBLE DON'T LAST

Trouble don't last always,

that's what I keep telling myself.

If I continue to believe,

God will do what's best.

I refuse to give in to doubt,

I will not stress!

This is only a test!

Trouble don't last always,

this is what I know.

My faith will stay in God,

this is what will continue to show.

Star Speaks

I STAND UP FOR ME

I stand up for me!

Now, what could this possibly mean?

Let's see....

I respect my true self,

I don't want to be anyone else.

Understanding my life has stages.

Some days are stories, others are pages.

As I grow,

along my journey I have seeds to throw.

It's my duty to make sure that they grow!

Expecting sunshine, rain, morning dew.

There's purpose in everything I go through!

I stand up for me,

my being is the meaning.

Star Speaks

RUNAWAY LOVE

She doesn't want to be hurt again,

So, she up & leaves at night when it rains.

Always leaving back a few remains,

only her name and a few memories.

She may have laid on your sheets,

so, you smell her fragrance.

Look under the nightstand, you might find her stash of

treats.

The only thing you did wrong,

was be what she needed in life.

Everything was right.

Until she felt you get too close to hurt her.

Insecurity in a child grew up to be an adult,

it's not your fault.

She liked you, cared for you, but it was too much for her.

She couldn't imagine living in a perfect world,

because she hasn't been the perfect girl.

One blink and it was through,

but she didn't want to hurt you.

·Star Speaks

BECAUSE I LOVE YOU

Because I love you,

I was there for you.

Stuck by your side,

made you feel my love,

see my love.

Touched your heart,

and your soul,

my soulmate.

Kissed your lips,

as well as your mind.

My love,

your love.

Your hurt,

my hurt.

I will always be there,

I'm still by your side.

Loving you always.

Remember me,

love me,

trust me,

I'm here.

Star Speaks

DESIGNER CLOTHES

The cost of my clothes don't define who I am.
I'm not impressed by the name on your hem.
I like to dress nice too,
expense just isn't my focus like it is to you.
My clothes tell a piece of my story,
and I don't want labels all over me!
To me, it's about freedom of creativity,
not label captivity.
I want to be unexpected chapter of a day.
Who knew you could wear clothes this way.
I spend money like I own it,
so, I don't blow it!
But I sure will stretch that bill,
all the way to the clearance heels.
Yes, I'll take last season's deals.
I'm the reason I'm surviving,
and I don't see them providing for me.
High designs won't ruin me!
I know how to live within my means, cause,
I'm cashing out on my dreams.
Not my account or my presidential greens!
When I step out, I still make the world scream!
Cause, I'm true to myself and what I feel to be!
Everyone checking for me,
waiting on the next chapter to be seen.

Star Speaks

<u>ALL I CAN</u>

All I can do,

is be what the great one designed me to be.

If I make a mistake, I am made to learn a lesson.

If I turn the wrong way, I just may find my blessing.

I treasure life's moments,

appreciate my gifts.

I'm thankful for what I do have,

even if there is struggle in my path.

Follow and live my dream,

feel what I say I mean.

And that's all I can promise.

*Star Speaks

LOVE HURTS

It's like no matter what,

I'll always feel this pain.

This emptiness,

that hurt,

the aching brokenness.

It's' like...

I'm in this space,

where I know things have changed.

Old feelings have also rearranged,

turning into new things.

I mean...

it's so hard to say,

I feel like I'm gonna burst!!!

How do you tell your love...

their love hurts?!

-Star Speaks

OUR FUTURE

As I look into his eyes,

I can tell...

that there's love,

passion,

hope,

commitment,

honesty,

mistakes,

rights and wrongs.

In his eyes,

I see mine.

Because, I look to him,

to see my future...

and he can't see his,

without me.

Star Speaks

I Believe

I started believing...

believing that...

I knew I would be right there,

up in the air,

but fall short.

I believed I would fail,

At everything I touched.

I believed they lied about...

my beauty,

my way,

my style.

But as I grew older,

I realized that I love me.

I love my eyes,

my complexion,

my scars,

my voice.

My soul,

my happy,

my nappy.

Me completely,

I believe it!

Star Speaks

<u>MY LIGHT</u>

He pulled me close,

held me tight & closer than most.

Listened to me fall apart,

while I'm pouring out things from my heart.

We're hearing things we've never said,

then he kissed me on my forehead.

Held me like he never had,

and it felt so right.

I'm in this tunnel but he's, my light.

Star Speaks

DANGEROUS IS SHE

I call her dangerous.

She loves you & keeps you,

feeds into your needs,

fulfills your fantasies.

She takes care of & loves your family,

so, you fall dangerously in love.

Keeping her to yourself.

Unreachable by anyone else.

So, like a rose in a bed of weeds,

she hides.

Tied and tangled,

suffocatingly strangled.

Still, I call her dangerous.

Because she rose up,

fought through death.

She took a step,

toward her life,

and her rights.

To be freed,

to be wildly creative & sincerely needed.

To be adored, pampered & appreciated.

Dangerous is she who has quality!

The lady who took a stand,

dangerous I am.

Star Speaks

DANGEROUS IS HE

Dangerous is he,
who is at peace.
The one who doesn't follow but leads,
a man who turns reality out of dreams.
I call him dangerous!
I trust him in his innocence,
feel comfort & relaxation in his kiss.
Got me in this space,
'cause, there's meaning in this man's face!
He's compassionate with his words,
so real it's unheard.
Compelled by his style,
suits up, beach bum to walk a mile.
Bottled my heart 'cause I'm Captured by his smile!
Dangerous is he,
who rocks with me.
Got me thinking could this really be?!
His journey to me, somewhat unknown.
Still, I'm thinking of making his home,
while he seeks the throne.
Cause, he walks with his head held high,
not so far that you can't see the passion in his eyes.
This one, this man...
dangerous isn't a part of his plan,
but he definitely is.
Dangerous is he who cherishes his kids,
the one with a plan,
this man takes a stand.

Star Speaks

MY BULLY

I was embarrassed...

of the way I looked,

where I lived,

and with who.

I was afraid of,

the emotions,

the elaboration of the things I dreamt.

I was my bully,

I bullied me!

Unraveled and unseen,

broken & unrelieved.

So, I prayed,

asked to be freed.

Faith replaced fear,

right then my meaning was clear.

Star Speaks

MY STORY

You don't know my story,

you've only read a page.

You don't know if I've been through,

or if I broke through!

You could be seeing my pain,

or it just might be my praise.

So don't look down your nose,

looking at me with a glare.

Tapping and telling your friends to stare,

because you're more interested in my binding.

The past that's behind me,

not the developing story ahead of me,

or the struggles of my history.

Judging me like your air is so fair.

Like your summary is written & clear.

You haven't even read my chapters,

or even know WHAT I'm after!

So don't just read my spine,

ready the story ENTIRELY!

Until you've read my history,

all you'll see is a piece of me.

Star Speaks

BROKEN BABY

Nineteen with a baby & broken heart.
Raising a baby with a broken spirit.
How am I like this?
My concentration and my focus,
It's so far off.
What's not is this baby crying,
my new alarm.
I used to hit my clock but this one I can't harm.
Holding him in my arms,
tears flowing,
I don't know what I'm doing!!
Please stop crying,
so overwhelmed I feel like I'm drowning,
why isn't anyone helping?!!
This child,
my child,
what could he learn from me?
I'm just a teen!
I don't even know what I want to be!
Why did God choose me?!
How can I show this baby what to be?!
I'm only a teen...
but...
my baby depends on me,
to help him grow strong.
I can do it,
I had it in me all along.
The love to spare,

I never knew it was there.
More important than my friends,
my nails, my hair...
Is a child that didn't ask to be here!
I'm a teen,
But my child will be my everything.

Star Speaks

FIRST THINGS FIRST

First things first,

I'm going to feed my family.

Some days smooth,

other days are worse.

One thing for certain,

God's got a plan & I've got a part!

I was a destiny from the start!

And what's for sure,

is that I'm meant for more!

But...

first things first.

Star Speaks

PRETENDER

He called her pretender,

the girl who wouldn't surrender.

The one with a mysterious appearance,

with a glow from a distance.

Hardcore face,

with a smile that lit up the place.

Country girl who spent some days in the city,

so angry but yet so pretty.

So graceful and pleasant,

but don't be fooled by her presence.

Who is this pretender?!

Why can't I reach her?!

She has her mind made up,

with a skin so ford tough.

As you watch her, you'll catch a glimpse,

of her inmate called freedom as she feels the music.

To figure her out would mean a lifetime,

but she won't let the guard down to let you inside.

She wants to let go,

but she just won't give up!

The pretender is her protector!

Star Speaks

<u>*TWICE REMOVED*</u>

How could I have thought...

he could ever love me?

How could I dream...

that I'd be his queen?

Why would it seem,

my worries would die?

Why do I believe...

I should ever be held high?

How with a love so tainted?

A heart so gated,

I couldn't even fake it.

My love was taken,

but no one replaced it.

My heart had been broken....

all to receive a token.

·Star Speaks

STEPS TURNED REAL

Seven years...

all it took was an hour to pack it all up.

With a face full of tears,

my time was up.

Carried him, I didn't,

gave him life I couldn't.

Loved him to be strong,

checked him when he was wrong.

Still...he constantly put up a fight,

but he slept good at night.

Cared for him, I did.

Gave effort because he was my kid.

Prayed for him, I did.

Put life into him, I did.

What are you supposed to feel,

when the steps turn real...

Star Speaks

HIS PURPOSE

His purpose is my plan,

I completely understand.

I'm blocking the noise,

and returned in a comforting voice.

Words of encouragement,

clearly heaven sent.

An understanding of what it meant,

no sweeter than the perfect kiss.

This is what I've dreamt!

My plan is his purpose,

I'll never be perfect.

The things I'm hearing...

that's my understanding.

Star Speaks

ULTIMATE FAILURE

Have you ever had a feeling of complete anguish?

Sounds like a clear foreign language,

of ultimate failure.

A horrible burden of pleasure,

a brokenness unfixable.

From shame to disgrace,

made to erase your face.

Off of his,

into his.

Destroying his name,

because you couldn't take the pain.

Interrupting his favor,

to replace it with glamor.

Rewinding what's on paper,

erasing what's been inked.

Quit, before you could think,

spoke before you wrote.

Read, before it was written,

taken, before it was given.

He says ask & it shall be given,

to those who will listen.

It's HE who is waiting,

for you to respond to your blessing.

Star Speaks

TODAY IS PERFECT!

I decided I wasn't going to wait,

I just needed to figure out what I'd take.

Going a million miles a day,

I was missing my break.

I decided the time was now,

I had to get up & fight!

It won't be easy; I can't lie down.

I have to push with all my might!

I decided that TODAY was perfect!

I have to take it; they won't hand it to me.

I have got to put this work in!

I WILL reach MY dreams, my goals, my destiny!

Star Speaks

SHARED LOVE

I wanna be loved.

I wanna be held & actually feel like...

I'll be alright.

I wanna be held for forever!

Not just for a night.

Be with my soul mate,

whom no one could ever take.

More than just a lover,

I'm one piece,

Their the other.

We belong together!

A kiss on my forehead,

shared dreams in our bed.

In spite of the world,

he's my man & I'm his girl.

Star Speaks

GOD WILLING

God willing,
the devil asking,
but he can't kill me.

God willing,
God allowing,
because he has always kept me.

God willing,
God seeking,
he's bringing me through.
I have his work to do.

God willing,
God fearing,
success is what I'm hearing.

Star Speaks

TURN RIGHT

He told me to see other people.

So, I took away my love,

but only in words.

I've got a heart attached to veins,

never to material things.

He always blew up my dreams,

so, I held onto love dreaming of what it brings.

Just in being.

And hopefully our meaning,

would describe the feeling.

What was he thinking?

Now wondering, if things turned right,

maybe he would've never left.

·Star Speaks

Yesterday has no say!

Yesterday has no say!

I made it to today anyway!

The devil tried me,

he thought he had me.

The song on my heart,

kept us apart.

Yesterday was just that,

I could've moved but instead I sat.

Waiting on his voice,

I couldn't have made a better choice.

The devil thought he stopped me,

hurt me to the point of bleeding.

What more can be said,

healing in a word clearly read.

Yesterday has no say,

God has me today!

Star Speaks

SLIPPED AWAY

I slipped away,

and that's the last thing he wanted.

What he really wanted was me,

but at the time, I had to wait.

If it were reversed that'd be messed up to say.

But have his way he did,

and waited for him,

I did.

Not intentionally,

not because I knew we were meant to be.

But because I needed to be freed.

To realize the wrongs he made,

he left when he should've stayed.

Now, he's ready for me,

but I slowly but surely, moved on.

Now, he holds me in his heart,

because my new man holds me in his arms.

Star Speaks

<u>CLEAR THINKING</u>

I hear the birds chirping,

and the frogs belting.

The sun shines upon my face,

nothing but God's grace.

Yesterday is a memory,

still a blessing in my history.

Thoughts untangled,

mind stayed on things I've dreamt.

Because my mind he decided would be kept.

Focused on statements made to make sense.

God, I'm so blessed!

I made it a point today,

to pray the pain away.

To take great steps,

God gave his, so I'll give my best.

Star Speaks

FILL IN

So, she walks in the place,

intending on getting a full set.

As she looks at the time she doesn't want to wait.

Clean em up,

file & smooth down the sides.

Remove what's fake, what kind of pain will it take?!

Please fill her in,

So, the fun can begin!

Polish em up,

give em that final look.

A couple of strokes was all it took!

Temporarily satisfied & she never looked twice,

out the door to find Mr. Right!

·Star Speaks

Invaluable lover

Invaluable lover...

the one that's wanted by many others.

Still...it's you that they are after.

Even if only to add to the story's chapters.

If only a night,

in their invaluable life.

A wrong made right,

sealed with a kiss and a hug so tight.

Just a memory,

in their invaluable history.

A season in their year,

a dosage of your remedy for cheer.

Invaluable lover chose you,

so whatchu gonna do?!

Star Speaks

BLACK & BEAUTIFUL

Black and beautiful,

just like you.

I'm breathing on the same air you're breathing.

Trying to heal the same wounds from which you

are bleeding.

Both wondering what our kids will be eating.

Here I go walking down the street & here's

another hating & not knowing a thing!

Mad at me, just full of jealousy 'cause I finally got

myself a piece of making it!

So, I'm taking it & thankful for it!

But I'm gonna stay black & beautiful!

Cause I'm breathing the very same air as you.

Getting salt thrown on the same wounds as you.

Just trying to do me.

Minding my business doing things peacefully.

But yet, you're still wasting time hating on me.

Cause I'm "that chick that thinks she's pretty".

Star Speaks

IF I...DON'T THINK...I'M BEAUTIFUL

If I don't think I'm beautiful, who will?

If I don't say it and claim it, who's gonna believe it?

If I don't believe I am good at what I do,

Why should others think this to be true?

I am just as fly as the next.

Try hard to be at the top like the best,

I've accomplished a lot.

I'm attractive & valuable,

I follow a path toward my destiny.

And I prepare for great things to happen for me.

I am beautiful no matter what I wear,

and no matter who's around.

I'm respectful and respectable,

I am beautiful & hopeful.

Hopeful of change in the self-worth of myself & others.

We are differently beautiful to each other.

*Star Speaks

WAIT...

He said he'd wait for me...

But what does that mean to me?

Putting on hold what someone else may need.

He's waiting for me when I needed to be freed.

What does this man see in me?!

The wild, crazy, shy, nice, mean piece of me.

Maybe, he really, truly loves me.

Completely,

Sincerely.

When I finally realized that the love, I wanted I just let go...

there's nowhere to turn.

He's already moved on to someone who promised,

she'd always hold on.

*Star Speaks

THAT DUDE

Back to that dude.

The one in a skirt,

light smiles and an attitude.

Little feelings and doing dirt.

Love is a word, not an action!

No ties, all movement,

no pics, just a reflection.

Slight stuff, no commitment!

All lines,

no passion.

They think they're close, all lies.

No truth, just reaction.

I'm back to that dude...

a little arrogance, a touch of rude.

Re-read what you think you see,

that dude... is me.

Star Speaks

HE'S HAPPY

I'm happy that he's happy.

Accepting love without me...

blending of families,

giving himself completely.

I'm happy he's found her.

Openly being his lover,

grounding & lifting him.

There's peace & love when you look at them.

I'm happy that our young, tough love,

grew into blessings of new love.

Truths, resolution & companionship.

Hugs, kisses & a strong relationship.

He's happy...

and it has nothing to do with me.

Honestly & surprisingly,

there is no jealousy.

I'm just happy...

That he's happy.

*Star Speaks

LOST

You may be lost,

but you will be found.

I'm so close if you'd just changed your noise,

and raise your ears.

If you bend a knee,

you could search for me.

If you've ever had a problem,

who have you called to solve them?

Because I've ALWAYS answered.

You're the one confused about your treasures.

I'll be around when you come get them.

*Star Speaks

GOD'S GIFTS

Who are you to hide my gifts?

To dibble and dabble in my treasures...

to ruin your mind,

trample my world.

To burn my tongue,

or bite my lip?

I am the creator!

You are the creation!

You are the process,

but I am the journey!

Who are you to hide my beauty?

To forget my struggle?

Not to mention my pain.

You can't return to me what I gave.

Walk in your mission,

use it to speak my vision.

To paint the picture,

adding focus makes it clearer.

People need to know I'm here!

My gifts bring more power than fear!

*Star Speaks

<u>ACKNOWLEDGMENTS</u>

Thank you!! Thank you!!! Thank you!!!!

I would like to thank **God** for blessing me with an outlet. One that has its own way (or his way) of teaching lessons. Of love, fear, heartbreak, trust and more. When I was alone, I found comfort in God.

Thanks to my **Ma, (Darlene),** for always having my back. Even when I didn't want to be helped. You just wouldn't let me fall! Thanks for holding me up when I was too weak to care. For your strength & unconditional love. The action of instilling values, the importance of hard work & family. Thanks for showing me what a strong woman looks like. Thanks for helping me through. You mean the world to me! Love you mostest.

My **Grandma Reese!!** For the positive and real outlook on things. The laughs, jokes and "Grandma don't play" demeanor. For believing in my gifts. For making me sing and recite my poetry when I was too afraid to. For understanding my crazy activity. My wild style and personality. Just for accepting who I was & am. The encouragement was & is appreciated. Love you mostest.

If you have purchased this book thank you so much!! I hope you enjoy your investment in my dreams!!!

I appreciate you all so very much!!

Star Speaks

Speak To Me

Email: Info@iamstarspeaks.com

starspeakskeepsakes@gmail.com

Social Media:

StarSpeaks or StarSpeaks Keepsakes

Facebook, Instagram, TikTok, YouTube

www.ingramcontent.com/pod-product-compliance
Lightning Source LLC
Chambersburg PA
CBHW071113090426
42737CB00013B/2586